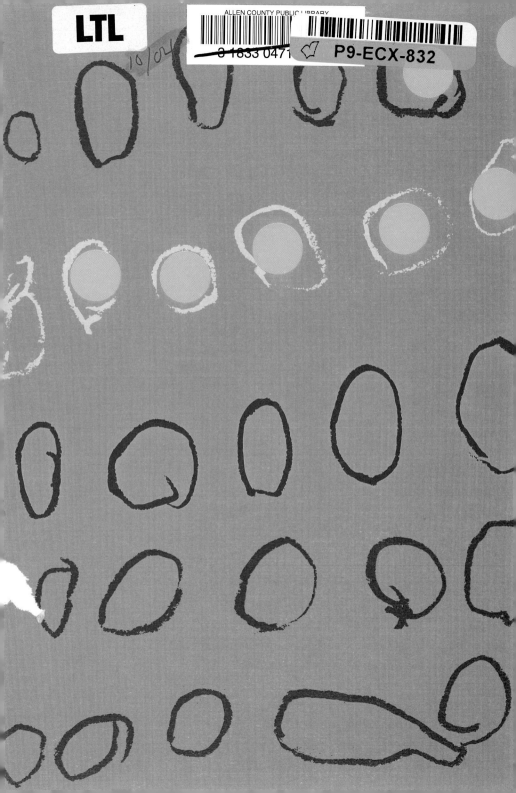

une
jolie
fleur
pour une
bien-
venue

AOACIO

cool kids' rooms

contents

Welcome to my world...this is my room!

Whether refined, bursting with color, sporty, whimsical or eclectic, the rooms on these pages share one common theme: imagination. Here, Parisian artists, designers and other creative professionals have opened their doors for an intimate glimpse into some of their most cherished creations—their children's bedrooms. Each room was designed with a special child in mind, yet with an individual flair that makes each a model of expression. With hundreds of ideas to choose from, this is your personal handbook to guide you each step of the way as you create your child's ideal abode.

Cassandre & Isé

A whole floor for Cassandre and Isé, designed with oodles of love.

Cassandre's favorite color is pink. So while work was under way, no shade of pink was spared! This roomy loft garret was 100 percent designed and furnished by Cassandre's parents, designer Mildred Simantov and architect Jérôme Liberman. The bunk bed, with a sloping space for hanging clothes (which Cassandre uses as a slide), was designed by Jérôme to fit perfectly into the existing contours of the space. The small round rug and felt baskets—perfect for storing toys—are Mildred's creations. To bring a magical atmosphere to her daughter's room, Mildred chose a string of colorful decorative lights playfully arranged on the wall to create an unexpected galaxy. A heart-shaped wall sconce insures that only sweet dreams are dreamt here!

Above: On Cassandre's stylish desk, her very own plant to take care of.
Opposite: In a limited space, toys are organized by type and stored in whimsical containers.

For one-year-old Isé's room, his parents chose a bright, sunny yellow for the walls with natural honey-colored wood furniture to blend with the parquet floors and enhance the room's natural warmth. Mildred extended her personal chic to every detail, coordinating even the gingham fabric for Isé's bed. To celebrate the arrival of her son, she made two very special presents: a picture that lights up for a night light and a portrait in acrylic to hang just above the changing table.

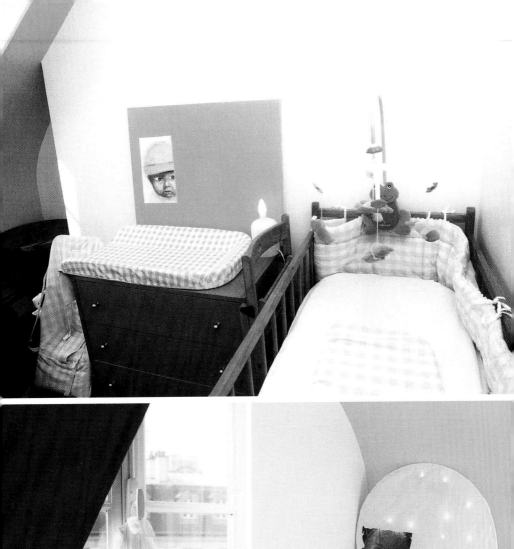

The apartment's top floor (three conjoined former maid's rooms) is earmarked exclusively for the kids. Between their two rooms the mezzanine landing has been converted to a small sitting room with cushions on the floor and a wall-sized beach scene. A small radio puts the finishing touches on the ambiance with sounds of the seashore.

Gabriel

Age: 4
Boy
Mom: illustrator

Gabriel is the envy of his buddies! His mom has loads
of great ideas to make a kid's life much nicer.

Gabriel's room was once his mother's studio. When he was born, the illustrator moved her pastels and brushes, but left all the telltale signs of her originality—from the ceramic objects on the shelves to the little table well stocked with everything needed to work on paper...and beyond!

Carlotta put her love of handicrafts to good use to custom-make everything a boy could ever need or want, including the gingham pillowcases and cloth bags with silk-screened motifs for Gabriel to store things all on his own. Even his photograph was retouched on the computer to become an original piece of pop art! There's plenty of space for Gabriel to grow into and being only four years old he'll soon need it. The room is spare enough that anything that Gabriel might need can be added. But right now, it's just perfect as it is.

Above: Lots of room for creativity, a little work table for art projects and a blackboard for scribbling whenever Gabriel feels like it.
Left: The banners and invitation cards designed by Carlotta for Gabriel's birthday were a huge hit with his friends. On the chairs, vintage children's shoes from the fifties add a homey charm.

Ninon

Age: 14 months
Girl
Mom: interior designer

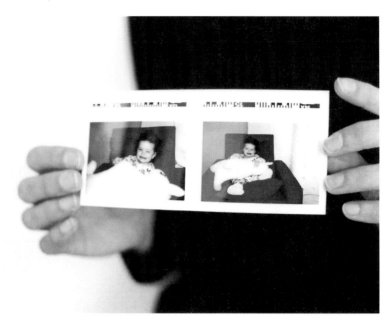

A love of bright colors and all things modern from a mom who is expert in matters of decor.

A very hip apartment, indeed, located near Paris's botanic gardens. For her daughter Ninon's room, Eva, an interior designer, opted for interesting juxtapositions. Natural materials mix with shiny plastics, brilliant white is enhanced with bright colors and contemporary pieces refresh secondhand objects. Everything here achieves harmony without reaching for perfection.

An expanse of yellow wall brings a warm contrast to a brightly striped carpet. Two seemingly mismatched chairs, one vintage fifties, the other plastic kitsch, make excellent companions. An enormous paper ceiling light sprinkled with delicate flowers empha-sizes the wonderful loftiness of this delightful little room, while the sun filters playfully through rows of cutout polka dots, dappling the floor with cheerful patterns of light.

Top: The wooden milk truck is a special hand-me-down—once Ninon's mom's favorite toy. Opposite; top, right and left: A duvet cover fastened with huge, colorful buttons and a felt curtain, handmade by Eva, full of playful cutout polka dots.

Hügo & Elliott

Ages: 5 and 3
Boys
Mom: publicist

Lots of room to play and a huge blackboard for creative self-expression—Hugo and Elliott are two lucky kids.

Fashion publicist Sandie Roy's three children have an ideal situation that works for everyone: Hugo and Elliott share one big room, while their big sister, Emma, has a smaller room all to herself. For the boys, their spacious room is many things at once—a football field, a playground and an artists' studio. Situated in a corner of the apartment, the room has an asymmetric shape and huge windows that flood the room with light. The room's spaciousness makes it ideal for play groups and slumber parties. Sandie knows very well what rowdy little boys are like and offers a very sound piece of advice when decorating a boy's room. "Since little boys will always be tempted to draw on the walls, why not indulge them by painting their walls with blackboard paint." That way they can have their cake and eat it too! A great solution for mom and kids alike!

"Do not flood the bathroom, eat only at the table, tidy your room...." If family rules are
followed, children are entitled to a little reward.

Emma

Age: 8
Girl
Mom: publicist

In nature-loving Emma's room, flowers bloom every-where—even on the comforter.

On the threshold of Emma's room, a riot of color rushes to greet you in an atmosphere of gaiety and fun. With a clever juxtaposition of objects from around the globe, her mom, Sandie, has created for Emma a simple yet delightful world.

To transform an ordinary bed, she hung a long, colorful beaded curtain in place of your average headboard and affixed two giant butterflies to the wall. Along with a glittery array of pillows and a gaily patterned duvet cover, the effect is feminine yet thoroughly modern.

A small lounging area is designated by a large plastic woven rug strewn with cushions covered in bright Chinese fabrics, where two unusual African carved-wood chairs hold court.

Emma's desk basks in the lovely light created by a sheer embroidered curtain. A perfect spot for a budding botanist's first garden.

Gustav

Age: 2
Boy
Mom: interior designer

Scandinavian style in soft colors creates a tranquil atmosphere for Gustav's room.

Like a castle turret in a fairy tale, Gustav's room is on the very top floor just beneath the rafters of this old converted barn. Although in Paris, Sweden is subtly evoked everywhere in this charming, airy room. Exposed wood, pastel colors and hand-crafted accents are the touch of Gustav's Swedish mother, Charlotte, who pays a lot of attention to atmosphere.

For her son, she wanted only the best: the softest rugs, fun—and functional—furniture and toys. With an expert's eye, Charlotte combed the garage sales for one-of-a-kind pieces that, with a little updating, became instant classics.

For a more personal feel, she improvised wonderful little touches—a clothespin line, a string of fairy lights, stenciled toy boxes—to make the room truly unique.

Above: These decorative yet functional shelves are Charlotte's handiwork, personalized with colored tape and yellow stickers.
Opposite: Tidying up was never this fun! Wooden bins were colorfully numbered with large stencils and bright shades of gouache.

Antoine & Pauline

Ages: 11 and 13
Boy and girl
Mom: design consultant

An urban atmosphere for Antoine's room; for Pauline, a stylish refuge under the rafters.

With its distressed gray finish, the parquet floor in Antoine's room evokes the asphalt streets where he loves to roller blade. Bright reds and blues with accessories of brushed aluminum all add up to a hip, urban look. Two big, bold cushions, sewn by Isabelle, Antoine's mom, transform the bed to a sofa when he has friends over—just like a real studio apartment!

To get to her private attic garret, Pauline climbs an old miller's ladder. This idiosyncratic room has so much natural character that a simple coat of white paint for the ceiling was enough to accentuate its dramatic contours while considerably brightening the space. A futon and a low, modern chest lend a bohemian style and pop-art shades of pink, orange and white put the finish on this chic, sophisticated look.

The long beams in this attic garret are a perfect spot to hang Pauline's favorite photos, drawings and mementoes. Contemporary touches contrast nicely with the room's natural rusticity to bring a very chic, Parisian feeling.

Welcome to Carla-Elle's bedroom—a budding artist who proudly displays her artwork on her very own "gallery" wall.

With two fashion designer parents—Isabelle Ballu and Moritz Rogoski—it's no surprise that five-year-old Carla-Elle already exhibits an impressive creative streak. And her room is her best work-in-progress. With an entire wall devoted to her drawings, Carla-Elle already has her very own gallery show. But that's not the only exhibit, from the precious 18th-century cushion fabrics to the painted insects on the wall, nearly every inch of this room has something interesting to look at.

Objects from the world over—like her stuffed Brazilian butterflies, dolls from Japan and Russia and a Chinese paper dragon—contrast with sleek contemporary touches: a hanging vase, cascading lights. All add up to a room that's one-of-a-kind.

Above and previous page: A simple made-to-measure wooden platform topped with a mattress, the bed is sleek and functional. The faux-fur bedspread provides a comfy spot for a sophisticated little girl's treasures—an array of fanciful teddy bears and Blythe, a vintage Japanese doll in a Mondrian-inspired pantsuit.

Opposite: Two nearly identical sepia photos of mother and daughter, then aged one, evoke another era (Carla-Elle affixed a beetle for her own personal touch). A Japanese school desk is dad's contribution, a bargain he couldn't resist for his beloved daughter.

Simon

Age: 8
Boy
Mom: illustrator

A sunny yellow hideaway with garden access for a world traveler who loves animals and the piano.

An old warehouse served beautifully for this eclectic living space complete with a garden. In Simon's room, stunning three-quarter-length windows overlooking the garden serve two important purposes: letting light in and letting Simon out!

Creamy yellow walls add warmth to this already bright space where the influence of Simon's illustrator mom is apparent in the abundance of artwork on the walls. Here art takes pride of place and Simon's drawings figure prominently next to his mom's, along with classic reproductions of favorite works. But the animal theme is the idea of the nature lover in the family. Simon also loves to display the many souvenirs of his travels. A marionette, a fearsome wooden tiger and curtains made out of a traditional sari—all from a recent trip to India—adorn the walls and give the room a colorful flair.

Left and above: One of Simon's favorite pastimes is to collaborate with mom, she draws his favorite cartoon characters and he colors them in himself. Tintin and Mickey Mouse have never looked more fresh and charming!

éopard se fit des

2001 Simon LEGAR

Casimir

For Casimir, the youngest of four, a pale, mint-colored room—like a cool breath of air.

The home of Stanislassia Klein, a common name in the realm of Parisian high fashion, lies just along the Parc des Buttes-Chaumont in the residential neighborhood known as "Little America." Rows of charming town houses lend this Parisian neighborhood a provincial feel—the perfect setting for Stanislassia's home, where the same subtle refinement and romanticism that characterize her collection hold sway. Her determination to instill a love of art in each of her four children (Casimir, Marguerite, Théodore and Anatole, whose rooms follow) inspired her to use a different, unique color for their rooms, along with precious pieces of furniture—some passed down through generations. For little Casimir, a fresh, subtle green suggests the hush of early spring, while a lovely mirror and comfy antique chair provide the perfect atmosphere for fairy tales.

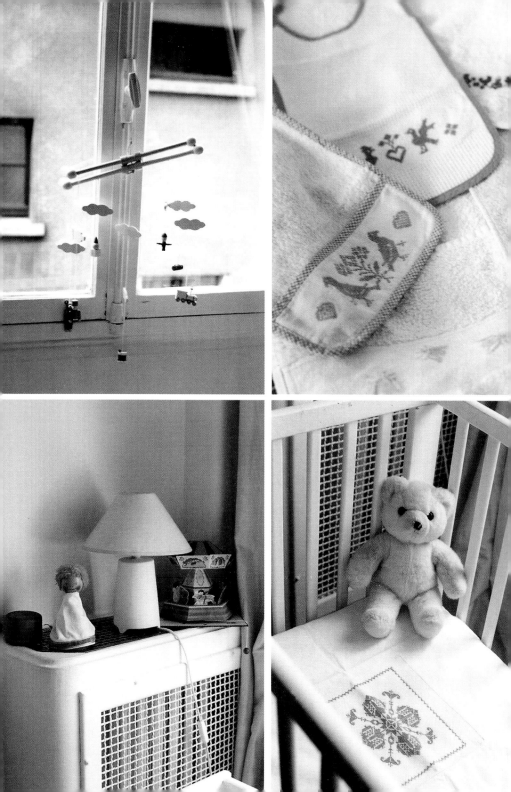

Above: This wooden chair belonged to Stanislassia when she was a girl.
Left: For each child's birth, Stanislassia's Ukrainian mother made unique hand-embroidered linens, like these bibs and cushion covers embellished with the simple motifs of her homeland.

Marguerite

Age: 9
Girl
Mom: fashion designer

Cotton-candy pink and burnished gold: a romantic fairy-tale atmosphere fit for a modern-day princess.

Marguerite loves to read; she also loves to draw, watch movies, and, like every nine-year-old, listen to pop music. She may love Britney Spears, but the eldest daughter of this household knows how to keep her cool. In harmony with the refined tastes of her fashion-designer mother, she confines posters of her favorite pop star to her bedroom door. The ethereal color of her bedroom walls, chosen by her mom at her birth, remains unchanged. The iron bed, once her grandmother's, went from black to the regal shades of ancient gold leaf; enhanced by a tulle canopy, this elegant bed looks truly majestic. To heighten the magic, Stanislassia (who knows all about enchantment) added pillows embroidered with angels' wings and a bedspread from her Stella Cadente collection trimmed with a row of light, silky feathers—no doubt from the angels themselves!

Marguerite seems to have inherited her mom's love of soft, feminine things; a display of baskets are as useful as they are charming. Her graceful antique writing desk is in keeping with the girlish theme—and its secret drawers deter curious little brothers!

Théodore & Anatole

For Théodore and Anatole a sedate lavender blue—as natty as an English banker's shirt.

Théodore and Anatole's room is simple and harmonious, inspiring a tranquility not often found in little boys, while still allowing them lots of room to romp and play. The ultra-refined lavender blue, chosen by Stanislassia when Théodore was born, is the ideal color for encouraging repose when the boys' get too rambunctious. Ice-blue plush carpet harmonizes the room, minimizing noise and giving the boys a soft place to land. For tidying up—a habit strongly advocated by their mother—there are plenty of options: transparent plastic boxes and decorative baskets with lids, ideal for holding precious dinosaur and dog collections. The generous bunk beds—a modern, streamlined design by their mom—also have two large drawers for storage. But the best thing of all is the lightweight top designed to fit between the bed and the desks to create their own private fort.

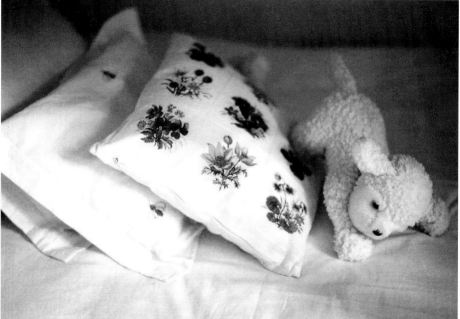

Top: Stanislassia keeps a tradition alive—at the birth of each child a silver tumbler was engraved with his or her name.
Above: Flowery pillows lovingly embroidered by Grandma to grace the boys' beds.
Opposite: Above their desks the portrait of a namesake—Théodore, their great-grandfather.

Marie

Age: 15
Girl
Mom: publisher

A teenager's hideaway with a view to the big wide world.

At the tender age of 15, is Marie already a world traveler? You might well ask yourself this question after seeing the colorful collage that is her bedroom. Part exotic bazaar, part flea market, part art gallery, this room is clearly the refuge of a very curious mind. Marie is a collector too and every inch of her room is occupied by an array of interesting curiosities and objects, each exhibited in its own special place. Even her beautiful aqua desk, painted by Mireille, her mom, is slowly being taken over by the treasures Marie collects on her trips abroad. Moroccan mirrors, Japanese pop objects, flashy Indian jewelry, all add up to a distinctly personal style. What are her favorite things? A glittering bedspread, a gift from a friend's trip to India, and a large curtain signed by André, the graffiti artist, a birthday gift from her mom.

Above: Even Marie's colored pencils show the thought and care that goes into this seemingly capricious arrangement.
Opposite, top right: Packets of bindis arranged just as they were in their last incarnation in India. Marie's desk, covered with tins of brilliant sparkling things, doubles as an exhibition space.

M ilo

Age: 2
Boy
Mom: stylist

Only two and already his name in lights! A great touch for a spare and stylish room.

Once a woodworking shop hidden away in the heart of Paris's Belleville section, Milo's uniquely shaped room was made-to-measure by parents well-versed in the art of do-it-yourself. For the floor they mixed a blue concrete, ideal for the wear and tear of an energetic toddler. Crisp white walls and transom windows that flood the room with sunlight keep the room bright and cheerful. Milo's mom, Sandrine, used lots of personal touches to contrast with the room's sleek, modern lines: polaroids of the important moments in Milo's life, along with drawings and postcards from friends and relatives commemorating his birth. Simple and functional, furniture streamlines the space, including some yard-sale treasures that with a coat of paint were easily transformed for a thoroughly modern look.

Sandrine loves the simple beauty of hand-made and traditional toys, including a charming Calder-esque mobile. On a shelf running the length of the wall, a delightful collection of toys, pictures and artwork tell the story of a little boy's happy life.

Acacio

Age: 8
Boy
Mom: illustrator

Aspiring young artist Acacio follows in his parents'
footsteps in an atmosphere of self-expression.

Acacio's home was not cast in the traditional mold. From the moment of his birth
he was surrounded with the trappings of an
artist's life. With both mom and dad in the
creative arts, Acacio's room makes abun-
dant display of the fruits of three fine tal-
ents. Perched in a third floor garret, this
wood-plank paneled room is covered nearly
floor to ceiling in artworks that run the
gamut from sophisticated to personal to
just plain funky.

Old engravings from flea markets, masks
and international objects, linocuts by Acacio's mom, Sophie, and Acacio's own pre-
cocious artworks make a wonderfully
colorful patchwork. All the iconoclastic fix-
tures and furnishings in the room were
flushed out of flea markets and country
auctions—the exquisite antique bed saw
its first course of duty in an abbey!

This little corner nook with Acacio's desk and chair serves as an artist's mini studio where he can have all the freedom he needs to express himself. His extraordinary surroundings attest to a confidence and imagination well beyond his years.

PARFOIS MON CORPS
SE PERD DANS CETTE VILLE.

ACACIO

Above: One of the more interesting drawings to be found on Acacio's walls is entitled "Girl and Her Guardian Angel."
Left: Around a large painting by his grandfather, another gifted artist, Acacio has hung his favorite drawings.

Lune

Age: 5
Girl
Mom: fashion designer

A real little girl's room with lots of pink and everything
soft and sweet.

With all the wisdom of her five years, Lune already has very clear ideas about what she wants. Even with a famously creative mom, designer Vanessa Bruno, Lune likes to make *all* the decisions for her room. First it must be pink, next there must be a real desk, just like at school, and when it comes to arranging, Lune knows exactly where things should go. Nevertheless, good-natured Lune has given her mom (who adores bargain hunting in flea markets) permission to add some of her best finds, such as a vintage Snoopy bedside lamp and a huge patchwork quilt decorated with barnyard animals. Lune also gives her mom carte blanche to bring back anything in the Hello Kitty series from her frequent trips to Japan. Tom, the house cat, is a frequent guest in Lune's room, but makes himself scarce when Lune's gaggle of friends arrive.

Top: This decorative towel printed with drawings by Lune's classmates was a Christmas gift.
Bottom: Lune loves the sneakers her mom brought back from New York so much that she's immortalized them in a portrait.

Joséphine

Age: 13
Girl
Mom: photographer

An up-to-the-moment mix of classical and modern shows Joséphine to be a girl in tune with the times.

In her two-story house in Paris's Latin Quarter, Joséphine's mom, photographer Marianne Chemetov, transformed a series of old offices into a spacious family home. While some parents adhere to the common wisdom of giving their children washable, unbreakable and otherwise practical furniture, Marianne blazed a new trail, filling her kids' rooms with antiques, fine fabrics and rare objects. She knows that doing so will teach them to respect and appreciate the finer things in life. In Joséphine's room a harmony of dark wood with natural hues and unusual furniture predominates. An antique sofa upholstered in raw linen becomes the prettiest of beds with Liberty of London floral sheets and a collectible quilt. Joséphine has plenty of ideas of her own, adding a necessary dose of the contemporary to her room with a dash of this and a pinch of that, all adding up to an elegant and sophisticated look.

Above: Torn between two great loves, painting and fashion, Joséphine takes drawing classes to hone her skills for the ultimate decision.
Left: Touches of glitter and color, like these Moroccan slippers, brighten up a classic room and add a touch of modernity essential to a girl who loves being à la mode.

Alexandre

Age: 9
Boy
Mom: photographer

In the style of a gentleman farmer, Alexandre's room has an elegant country look in the heart of the city.

A large neoclassical bed that might have served one of Napoleon's soldiers; a splendid armoire in trompe-l'oeil wood grain; a country doctor's desk...all add up to a signature look for Alexandre's room, much different from his sister Joséphine's. There was a lot to work with in this classic room with its tall ceilings and creamy walls. From the magnificent parquet floors to the dramatic floor-to-ceiling shutters, it's the wood in all its various patterns and shades that creates an elegant, warm and inviting bedroom. Mom's keen eye for finding just the right pieces of furniture in her forays to the local flea markets and antique shops is evident in the juxtaposition of old and new. A timeless feel reigns in this unusual home, but in Alexandre's room, for all its sober elegance, his personal things (he loves horses and soccer) help create a pleasant lived-in quality appropriate to a boy's room.

Top: Alexandre's impressive miniature animal collection gets its very own Noah's ark on a tabletop perfectly suited for the job.
Opposite: An imaginative use for an old kitchen shelf that hold lots of little things in a tidy array.

Margot & Lili

Ages: 9 and 7
Girls
Mom: illustrator

Walk into Margot and Lili's room and enter a colorful comic strip abuzz with energy and vitality.

Margot and Lili are the best of friends, and they adore their cozy little room so snug under the attic rafters. Every square inch of this diminutive room was utilized in the most ingenious manner: Made-to-measure shelves hold just about anything two little girls could need, and the built-in cupboards fit perfectly under a slanted ceiling painted white to accentuate the beautiful exposed beams. Patches of bright color stand out amidst the predominant white in surprising places like the back of the shelves in a lovely raspberry red and stripes of deep blue above the storage units and on the wall where their desks sit to offset the light that floods in through the attic window. Each and every item seems to have its place and there's still room for plenty of whimsey and fun in the drawings painted right on the wall, a gift from their talented mom.

Above: A long desk with lots of light serves both girls, perfect for homework, put even better for drawing and painting.
Left: Mom is entitled to draw on the walls, not just because she's Mom but because she's a talented illustrator whose lively drawings brighten up the interstices of the room.

Margot and Lili's colorful and humorous pictures once decorated a present for Mom, a long-standing tradition since the girls were small.

Siméon & Marthe

Ages: 5 and 10
Boy and girl
Mom: designer

A riot of primary colors, Siméon and Marthe's rooms are a cross between a playground and a circus.

Siméon and Marthe's parents, Paul and Sophie, transformed an old artist's atelier in Paris's Belleville neighborhood into a gracious little home. With large doors opening onto their own private courtyard, the children can play happily on the very doorstep of their rooms, which are conveniently placed right next to each other. In each room an original use of color accentuates the high ceilings and large windows (a characteristic of an old craftman's studio), with a thin stripe of blue to define the upper and lower regions. The painted concrete floors have been cleverly decorated with world-map-motif linoleum cutouts that match the furniture's primary colors. A patchwork quilt and brightly colored toys, fabrics and accessories add up to a festive atmosphere in these unusual rooms.

Above: In Siméon's room, a large orange kite covering the ceiling light softens the height of the room. Carryalls designed by Paul and Sophie hang decoratively (and usefully) on a hook—the red cotton bag with a car patch was specially made by Sophie for her son.
Left: Total freedom of artistic expression is encouraged in this playful space where the kids rule!

Above: Siméon and Marthe's handiwork is displayed among the toys on the walls and shelves of their bedrooms.
Left: With doors opening right onto a sunny courtyard, as soon as warm days arrive the children can play or snack outside.

Angèle & Oskar

Ages: 7 and 4
Girl and boy
Mom: artist

A shared room lovingly (and exquisitely) designed by some very gifted adults.

Illustrator Nathalie Lété designed the lion's share of things in her children's room; from the patterned curtains to the comforter covers and even some of the toys. For the overall design of the space she had some very distinguished help from architect Pierre Roch and from her husband, painter Thomas Fougeirol. Situated on the second floor of the family's loft, Angèle and Oskar's room was designed with harmony and symmetry in mind. Rather than the usual bleak wall, they installed a large glass door and partition that opens onto the corridor and gives the room a sense of openness and light. A voluminous curtain with appliqued motifs spans the partition and insulates the children from noise and light when they're trying to sleep. The logic here was to design up, stacking storage units and shelves to leave plenty of floor space for the kids to play.

Above: Oskar likes to climb the ladder to reach his bunk. For Angèle's bed, Nathalie made a pretty canopy in a checked cotton fabric. A small wooden medicine cabinet was suspended from the wall to make an unusual night table.

Left: Nathalie's prolific imagination can be found in nearly every aspect of the room—from the fanciful curtain design to the cuddly knitted animals that the children adore.

A special little cabin all her own—as lofty as a tree house but much more inviting!

This mini-studio is like a little house nestled within a house—requiring three flights of stairs to reach it! In this block of former artist studios in the Montparnasse neighborhood of Paris, the bohemian atmosphere has clearly regained its stature. The buildings themselves carry a fascinating imprimatur—they were built with the scaffolding timber cast off from the Eiffel Tower. Nina's room fits right in, with a little help from her interior designer mom who collected soft, flexible materials in bright modern colors for Nina's furniture and accessories. Mom also chose white for the walls and parquet floors accented with striped or brilliantly colored rugs to lighten this little aerie. Large posters, flowers and drawings add vibrancy to the atmosphere of an artist's garret perched in the sky!

Creativity runs in the family: Nina's grandfather is a graphic artist and her mom an interior designer—their expertise in color and design is clearly evident in her room.

Léo & Paul

Ages: 10 and 4
Boys
Mom: publisher

A large minimalist space with plenty of room for the boys' fun and games.

Publisher Marie-Odile Briet and illustrator Hervé Tullet have transformed this three-floor former hotel into an accommodating home for themselves and their three children—and, of course, Maki the cat. On the top floor, Léo and Paul share the largest, brightest and most fun room of all. The room seems to have been given over entirely to sport and play: A smooth concrete floor, with a surface not unlike the streets where they love to skateboard, makes the best of playgrounds. Lots of storage space in shelves and drawers of various shapes and sizes help keep things tidy. The rooms' skylights give it a boxing-ring effect around which is arrayed furniture salvaged from yard sales or inherited from grandparents. But most of all, it's a place for kids, perfectly adapted to the energetic activities of young boys.

Top: Léo and Paul are happy to share a desk. But when it comes to drawing, their dad's studio on the first floor is the destination of choice.
Left: With the influence of two creative parents, there's always a little exhibition of the children's pictures on view.

Lucie

Age: 2
Girl
Mom: publisher

Bright tulip yellow and golden wood for a little girl as lively as a summer's day.

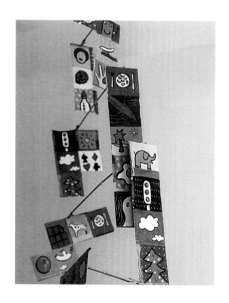

Before Lucie's birth, this room was her illustrator dad's studio. But when their first daughter was born, Hervé and Marie-Odile wanted her to have a cozy room all her own that she could grow into and chose the studio for Lucie's bedroom. To brighten up the space, which was short on light, they chose a warm tulip yellow with highlights of white for the ceiling and the little cubbyholes in the walls. With the color in place, Lucie's parents had a wonderful time supplying the finishing touches: Marie-Odile went sleuthing through all kinds of flea markets, antiques stores and rummage sales, to find interesting and unusual touches like a collection of colorful paper suitcases and a set of doll's heads. Hervé took a more personal route creating many little custom-made masterpieces, bright and cheerful for a sweet little girl's room.

Above: In the midst of these tiny treasures the best of all is a whimsical one-of-a-kind night light, created specially for Lucie by her loving and talented dad.

C éleste

Age: 4
Girl
Mom: interior designer

La vie en rose for Céleste? Absolutely!

No sooner had they moved into this large house close to the Bois de Vincennes, than the parents of Céleste, Faustine and Louise began renovation on the girls' rooms. Each was repainted white, then their decorator mom, Pauline, helped each daughter choose her favorite color to then be featured on one wall of her room. Céleste, like many girls her age, chose bubblegum pink! A perfect choice, it turned out, as it brought out the lovely highlights in the old marble fireplace and gave a soft rosy light to the room. With the leftover pink paint they spruced up a desk Céleste inherited from her big sisters. To protect the wall behind it, Pauline placed a wooden board on which little girls can draw to their heart's content and then hang the fruits of their labor. Two brightly checked scalloped curtains filter the light from the large windows and little round rugs bring old parquet floors up to date.

Above: Next to Céleste's ample bed, with drawers for storing all her toys, the iron radiator blends in with the rosy pink wall.
Left: A sleek Russian rocking horse was a gift from Céleste's grandparents.

Faustine

Age: 9
Girl
Mom: interior designer

Faustine's colorful and innovative room—an expression of the girl herself.

Faustine knew she wanted yellow. "Her aesthetic sense sometimes takes different directions than mine," says her interior designer mom. But in her room Faustine is the one who decides and she chose a brilliant sunflower color. So to complement the warm, sunny atmosphere of her newly repainted room, Faustine and her mom agreed upon accents of red and orange. For example, a thick curtain of red chenille, with a cheer white undercurtain to let daylight in. The cheerful orange polka-dot carpet helped bring the classic parquet floors and fireplace up to date and supplied a central motif in the room, showing up on a lampshade in inverse colors and elsewhere throughout the room. Two large moon-shaped sconces flank the fireplace and Faustine's favorite posters, pictures and drawings add the final touches to complete the envisioned look.

Polka dots are an important theme in Faustine's room and can be found scattered about in all kinds of places. On her desk and shelves even her goldfish become a design element.

Louise

Age: 7
Girl
Mom: interior designer

As fresh as a Mediterranean morning, turquoise blue gives Louise's room a wash of tranquility.

A fresh blue, somewhere between a tropical sea and a peppermint cordial, was Pauline's contribution to her daughter's desire for blue. Rather an easygoing girl, Louise was delighted with her mom's proposals for the redecoration of her bedroom—as long as she had carte blanche to display her horse posters, her one great passion. But the real challenge for the room was to find solutions for storing and displaying all Louise's things, Louise, you see, hates throwing anything away. So with various innovations—a clothesline to hand postcards, drawings and her lucky charms, a long hanging shelf next to her desk and shelves of various shapes and sizes—Louise's room is as orderly as mom and daughter like it. The mantelpiece also provides a perfect spot for treasured mementoes and a hopscotch rug gives Pauline hours of fun when she can't play in the park.

Above: A modern wardrobe fits next to the fireplace whose mantel makes the perfect display for Louise's important treasures.
Left: For a ceiling light the unexpected, a large transparent bucket that can be filled with whatever strikes her fancy. In this case large tarlatan, patches matching the polka-dotted duvet cover.

Resources

FURNITURE, BEDDING & ACCESSORIES

Babiesrus.com
Furniture, bedding, accessories.
Several locations throughout the U.S.
www.babiesrus.com

Bellini
For infants to teenagers.
Cribs, strollers, custom bedding, curtains.
Nine stores located in California, three in Texas, one in Nevada, one in Washington.
www.bellini.com

Buy Buy Baby
Cribs, changing tables, toy chests, lamps, rugs, bedding sets. Big kids' rooms.
Seven stores located on the East Coast (all stores can accommodate
phone orders; can ship anywhere in the continental U.S.).
1-516-507-3417 / www.buybuybaby.com

Ethan Allen Kids
Beds, headboards, canopies, dressers, chests, night tables,
bookcases, desks, cribs, bedcoverings, lighting, rugs.
Over 300 stores throughout the U.S., Canada and abroad.
www.ethanallen.com

IKEA
Beds, tables, chairs, highchairs, storage, cribs, changing tables,
rugs, lighting, toys, textiles.
Many stores throughout the U.S., Canada and abroad.
www.ikea.com

Pottery Barn Kids
Girls' and boys' bedrooms, nurseries, studies, storage,
bedding & bath, rugs, windows, toys.
Several locations throughout the U.S.
1-800-993-4923 / www.potterybarnkids.com

TOYS

Toysrus
www.toysrus.com

FAO Schwartz
www.fao.com

CLOTHING FOR KIDS OF ALL AGES, FROM INFANTS TO TEENAGERS

Benetton Kids
Several locations throughout the U.S.
www.benetton.com

Gap Kids & BabyGap
Several locations throughout the U.S. and Canada.
www.gap.com

Gymboree
Several locations throughout the U.S. and Canada.
1-877-4-GYMWEB / www.gymboree.com

Oilily
Several locations throughout the U.S.
1-800-977-7736 / www.oililyusa.com

Talbots Kids
Over 800 stores throughout the U.S. and Canada.
1-800-992-9010 / www.talbots.com

The Children's Place
Several locations throughout the U.S. and Canada.
www.childrensplace.com

Nordstrom
Several locations throughout the U.S.
www.nordstrom.com

Bloomingdales
Several locations throughout the U.S.
www.bloomingdales.com

Neiman Marcus
Several locations throughout the U.S.
www.neimanmarcus.com

Because the rooms featured on these pages are in private homes, all the items pictured may not correspond to those available in our resources guide. We offer only an approximate listing of widely accessible shops where the likelihood of finding similar items is greatest. The editors do not endorse any of the products mentioned or pictured.

The team

Art direction: Hisashi Tokuyoshi for Jeu de Paume

Photographs: Hisashi Tokuyoshi

Layout: Megumi Mori, Tomoko Osada

Texts: Fumie Shimoji and Coco Tashima (Japan)

Coordination: Takaaki Suzuki (France)

Editors: Vanessa van Zuylen and Sophie de Taillac for Editions de Tokyo Paris

U.S. edition

Translation: Simon Pleasance and Fronza Woods

Layout: Maria Maramzina

Copy editing: Jennifer Ditsler-Ladonne

ISBN: 2-05010-024-7

Printed in France

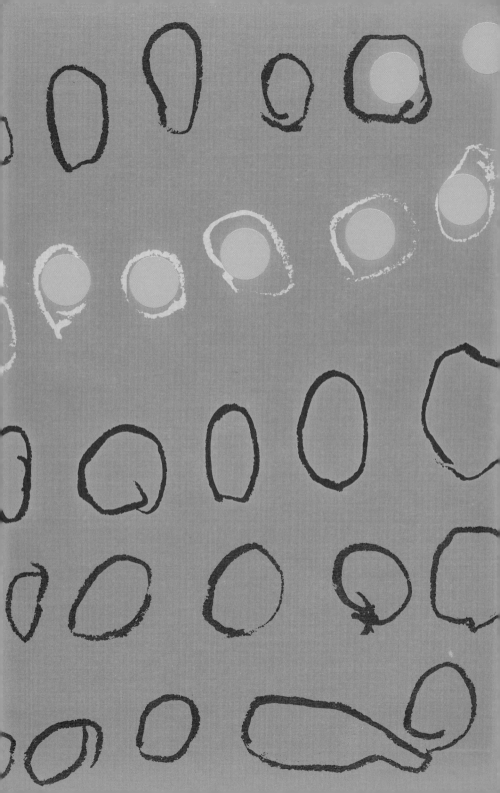